POETICSITUATION

POETICSITUATION

NOEL JONES

ISBN-13: 9780692613092
ISBN-10: 0692613099

PREFACE

Poetry makes the heart, mind, and soul... Dance to the beat of words.

- Noel Jones

Dedication
To my Mother who raised me right.
To my Husband who always believes in me.

TABLE OF CONTENTS

INSPIRATIONAL SITUATIONS

I want to live my life the way that GOD planned.
What he mapped out for me with His own hands.
To be who GOD wants Me to be.
To see what GOD wants Me to see.
To hear what GOD wants Me to hear.
To always feel His Presence near.
I don't want to have hate in my heart,
or let my flesh keep Us apart.
I don't want to be ignorant of his word,
Or cut off from the blessings that I deserve.
I want to give and receive love.
Show affection, kiss, and hug.
I want to make a difference, a change.
Say Yes to GOD when He calls my name.
To remember to lift my neighbors up.
To keep the faith and never give up.
When I'm going through something that I don't understand,
To remember It's all a part of GOD's plan.

2.
Lord, today please bless my family and all those close to me.
May our day be joyous and your love surround us.

3.
GOD knows that we all make mistakes.
That's why He gave Us a way to escape.
We are forgiven you and me, Saved by GOD's love and mercy.

4.

I have the faith of a Mustard seed.
My GOD shall supply all of my needs.
I know that He hears my Prayers.
In the midst of turmoil, He's always there.

5.

As GOD makes the Sun rise.
He also awakens Our weary eyes.
Overnight He has kept thee.
Another day He has granted me.

6.

It's Harvest time-!
Blessings are mine.
I've sown my seeds.
I've done my good deeds.

7.

Live your Life as if your already where you want to be.
GOD has already fully equipped thee.

8.

I was asleep, sound asleep
I couldn't hear a peep.
Mind free of chaos
Not worried about the "what Nots".
Then suddenly rain came pouring down.
Then I heard this trembling sound.
I was awakened by the Earth shaking.
Then the thunder started to roar.
I saw lightning like I had never seen before.
Yet I felt a calmness come over me.
Peace, joy, and tranquility.
At first I thought that I was still asleep.
Then I heard the most beautiful music ever.
Pianos, harps, and strings synchronized together.
Slowly the sky began to open up wide.
For some reason I got anxious inside.
Was this the day? Was this the place?
Am I about to meet my Maker face to face?
All these years that I believed.
My Savior I was going to see.
I saw a glimpse, then looked away.
What would you do if you saw Jesus today?
Would you welcome Him in? Or run away?
Be scared of Him? Or give Him Praise?

MESSED-UP SITUATIONS

Mama please,
Mama please don't whoop me.
Don't make me pick a switch off the tree.
Mama please don't fuss and fight.
Don't leave me alone again tonight.
Mama please try to understand, you are someone without a man.
Mama please don't leave the key underneath the mat
The whole neighborhood knows where it's at.
Mama please leave the drugs alone
Without you here this house is not a home.

2.
Depression is a dark place.
Love and self-worth diminish without a trace.
Illness consumes the soul, mind, and body.
Causing one to jump free from misery.

3.
I haven't smiled in a while.
Nor have I laughed in the past.
My tomorrows are full of sorrow.
My years are full of tears.

4.
Yesterday I felt like giving up.
Poured Jack Daniels in my cup.
Today I woke up with a migraine
Still trying to sip away the pain.

5.

I was doomed from the womb.
A preemie, born two months too soon.
All because of cigarettes.
Mom still smoked while she was pregnant.

6.

They swoon around.
When I got my spoon around
Got plenty of friends
Until the party ends.
Injecting myself, crying out for help.

7.

I was put here just for you.
To lie, cheat, even deceive you.
To make you feel like I'm your best friend.
To make you think I'm here until the end.
I want you to crave me, until you can't live without.
You'll soon love me without a doubt.
I'll make you feel stronger than Superman.
If anyone can do it, you know that I can.
Once you get a hold of me, you'll never let go.
The dealers get rich and the addicts get po'.
You'll lose weight, your job, your entire family.
But who needs them when you have me.
They all just tripping, they don't know
Just how much you love me so.
I do something that triggers the brain.
One hit buddy and you'll never be the same.
Oh sure, at first it was just for fun.
But your life with me has just begun.
I'll take you to new heights you've never been to before.
Next thing you know, you're out trying to score.
Only you don't have a regular supplier, got robbed of a hundred dollars.
Now you have no more money, thinking about selling your honey.
You want me and you want me bad.
Willing to sale everything that you ever had.
I sit back, I watch, and I laugh.
Watching your Sprung ass sell everything that you have.

MEDIA SITUATIONS

A billion dollars on the elevator,
Jay, Solange, Beyoncé, keep it together.
Got to keep your Brand going strong,
Smile and act like nothing's wrong.

2.
I use to want to be a fly on the wall,
but the fly in the elevator hears it all.
From Ray Rice knocking out his Fiancé.
To Jay, Solange, and Beyoncé.

3.
I guess It's official
Adam and Steve
Amanda and Eve.

4.
I do regret being 16 and pregnant
Didn't look like this on TV.
Never saw this episode of MTV.

5.
Turned on the TV,
To Jerry, Jerry.
Topic today
Results of the DNA.
Do your dance bad boy
......The kid is not yours.!

6.

Brenda is not the only girl having babies
It's Lisa, Mounique, and Mercedes.
It seems like the latest thing
Is having babies without a wedding ring.
I love my baby daddy and he loves us.
Weddings are just a bunch of fuss
No papers are just fine for us.
Half-sisters and half-brothers
Everyone is related to one another.
Taking that risk to infect one another.
Breast feeling tender and stomach getting bigger
Now all of the sudden baby daddy don't remember.
Swore that he wore a condom, says he wasn't the only one.
Next thing you know baby daddy is gone.
Now forced to apply for public assistance
How's $380.00 gonna pay the rent?
Before I get it, it's already spent.
To supplement I got to apply for WIC.
Jr's getting older, the streets are getting colder.
Baby daddy had another child
Haven't heard from him in a while.

RACIAL SITUATIONS

Don't judge me based on pigmentation
Or frown upon my Cocoa complexion
Get to know my character within
Not just the color of my skin.

2.
When I go to the restaurant with "William"
I get seated with a smile.
When I go with "Will-Dog" I have to wait a while.
Why is that?
Because William is white and Will-Dog is black

3.
It's crazy in L.A.
The kids can't come out and play
Drive-By shootings night and day
Tell me, how are the kids supposed to play?
Police harassing all black people
They don't treat us like an equal

4.
Officer, Officer
Quick, quick, quick
The robbers are getting away
Take out your stick.
Him, right there with the blue eyes
Not the dude that's chillin' in his ride.
While your Profiling racially
I'm searching for equality.

I guess you got side tracked
Assumes the suspects are black
Officer, Officer
Put away your gun
Those kids are only trying to have fun
True, you don't like the music that they play
Hell, they'll only end up in jail anyway.
Take them off the streets and lock them up for good.
Give them some Heat, watch them tear up their Hood.
Put about two or three liquor stores on the corner
Especially in South central California.
While you're at it, better add some churches
A mortuary with at least six hearses.
Officer, Officer
Please come fast
Someone took my purse with all of my cash.
Him right there tall and blonde.
Yes I'm sure, I can't be wrong.
No Mr. Officer listen to me
Now you want my I.D.?
I'm the one that called you, show some respect
Now all of the sudden I'm a Suspect.

5.

Men in Blue
Please stop killing our Youth.
Our kids are dying over Skittles and hoodies
Police officers are the main Bullies.

6.

What if Mike "Brown"?
Was Mike "White"?
Would He still be alive?
If He had blonde hair and blue eyes?

7.

I did mourn, for the Officers in uniform.
Now "Men in Blue" who's protecting you?
It's all one big disaster
All Lives Matter.

8.

We can change the world
One step at a time.
It all starts with the renewing of our mind.
Putting away hatred, malice, and greed
Fighting for all races and creed.

SITUATIONS OF THE HOOD

You say that you hate stereotypes
But then you go and prove them right.
You preach non-violence
But then you go and fight.

2.
What I used to get teased about
Is now being pleased and sought
I never thought I'd see the day
When Ass could be bought.

3.
I went and got a new set of girls
A low cut blouse and a string of pearls.
I walked over to the local bar
Thinking I should have bought a car.

4.
Ghetto Princess
If it don't make dollars, it don't make sense.
Beauty on the outside
Don't come at me sideways
Earned my crown, jewel of the town.
May look innocent, but I will throw down
Born of hustlers who run this city
Thick, luscious, and hella pretty
Bow down when you see me
Rolling down the street
You ain't my friend if you ain't my peeps

Cold-blooded, hot lover
Ghetto Princess is taking over.

5.
Yes I'm pretty
Don't get it twisted.
May look gentle
But I can get wicked
Fair skin, Good hair
Think twice before you stare.
Wha'cha looking at?
Yes I'm all that.
Stare too long you may get slapped.
High heels, designer clothes
Cadillac's and low-low's
Don't hate, Appreciate.
I keep it real, never fake.
Sculptured nails, triple beam scales
9-to-5, late night sales
Mother, daughter, wife
Street soldier for life.

NOEL JONES

6.
Yesterday I went shopping because I was bored.
Ended up buying shoes I couldn't afford
Today I was a little depressed
So I went out and bought a dress
Thank God for American Express

7.
It's costing me more to be me every day.
Have to portray me like they say
Have to drive a Range or a Benz
Just to end up with some fake ass friends.

8.
Don't wear your wealth
On the Name brands of someone else
Don't waste your cash
On designer hand bags
You knew when you bought those Red Bottoms
That you could not afford them

9.
With all the hustle, bustle, and grind
I'm about to lose my mind
Steady trying to climb the ladder
Forgetting what really matters.

SITUATIONS OF THE HEART

I'm a little crazy
But He gets me.
My smart ass mouth, He thinks it's witty.
My crooked smile, He thinks it's pretty.
He knows that I'm not perfect, and I don't have to be.
For He loves me for me.

2.
When God made you He broke the mold
A fine young man with a heart of gold.
When God made you He took His time.
A Love like yours is hard to find.
When God made You He created Himself
He knew I could never love anyone else.
When God made You He smiled with glee
He created You just for me.
When God made you, He had me in mind
Because He knew I'd love you until the end of time.

3.
They say age ain't nothing but a number
Have they ever took out the time to wonder?
That true love is patient and kind.
Real love surpasses all time
You're only as old or young as you feel.
It does take time for all wounds to heal.
Each day is the beginning of something new.
Not promised to me, not promised to you.

4.

Just because we are of the same gender.
Does that mean that I can't love you tender?
Physically we are one in the same
Society pushes ignorance and shame.

5.

Men shower your Woman with kisses and hugs before the next man does.
If you truly want her, compliment and flaunt her.

6.

I use to fear that he would steer every time that he left here
That's just me, being Insecure.

7.

I use to be your baby
Now it's more like maybe
I use to be your Boo
Now it seems were through
I use to be your sweetheart
Now it seems were growing apart
I use to be the love of your life
One day even your wife
I use to be your baby girl
Now it seems Our love has failed
I use to be your Only one
Now I wonder if I'm number one.
Use to call me every night
Now you say that you might.
Use to be your sunshine
Get you drunker than fine wine.
Now it seems you don't drink at all
Your thirst for me has suddenly stalled.

SELF-LOVE

I Say No, not because I'm too shy
I Say No, Not because I'm too Fly
I Say No, to simply say Yes.
Yes to Life, Yes to being a Virgin wife.
Yes to a deeper relationship
Yes to the meaning of a real passionate kiss
Yes to Self-Control, not depending on birth control
Most importantly I Say No for me
I choose to live a lifestyle of Celibacy.

2.
Today I confronted my Flaws
I actually liked what I saw
From the Scar on my left check
To the corns on my feet
I finally Love who I see.

3.
God gave me Curly Locks
So that's what I got
No need to spend money on straightening products.

4.
I use to yearn for "Good" hair and light skin
Dreading my own dark skin
Now I embrace my dark skin
My Light and beauty within

5.

I'm a mixed chick in a black and white world
My daddy black, my mama a white girl
Society tries to label me as "Other"
I too Am a Woman of Color

6.

I shine like a Beacon
So strong it makes Him weaken
Like a hot melted candle
My light he cannot handle
I will not dim my glare
So He can stare
My light is mine
Forever I'll shine.

7.

My Afro, Big and Black
My derriere Big and Stacked
My word is bond
My head is strong
My Afro, Big and Black
I choose to wear it like that
I choose my own destiny
It's all up to me
My Afro, Big and Black
I've learned to believe in all of my dreams.
My Afro, Big and Black
It's not where I'm from but where I'm at
My Afro Big and Black
No Hot comb for me
No silicone for me.

SELF-HATE

I show no love because I'm heartless
I have no manners because I'm thoughtless
I rep my hood because I'm Cowardless
I shoot my gun because I'm powerless
! feel no remorse because I'm cursed
Yes Indeed cursed from a seed
Born to die for my color, you know the deal
I can't love my brother, you know the real
Don't let his rag be of another color
That is a recipe for murder
I'm willing to go against my own people
To prove Red and Blue aren't equal
It's worth a trip to the county morgue.
To prove my color is better than yours.

2.
How to get rid of a Black man for good
Sell them some guns, watch 'em tear up they hood
Make them fight over Colors
Make them Kill one another

3.
Gang Banging is alive
Yet more Black men die
Street soldiers with ambition and ammunition
Loyal Goon
Gone way too soon

STICKY SITUATIONS

Commissary, Collect calls
Too familiar to us all
Stay strong it won't be long
Until you're hearing that freedom song

2.
So the Man's got you locked up
That's pretty messed up.
Don't they have better things to do,
than keep on messing with you?
You didn't even do Nothing
Well, maybe a little something, something.
Keep your head up, there is always hope
And remember….. Don't drop the soap.

3.
Looks like the Judge had a grudge
A lighter sentence He did not budge
I know right now things look down,
and that smile is now a frown..
In times like this, when life seems unfair
Just take it up to God in prayer.

POETIC ADVICE

You can't hang with chickens and soar like an eagle
In life you must cut of certain people
Don't let your friends
Keep you caged in.

2.
Not everyone will want to see you shine.
They only see the glory and not the grind.
.... Still I Rise.

3.
Don't measure yourself based upon riches and wealth
But by the Peace, love, and joy
You have within yourself.

4.
Words are shaper than a sword
What are you doing with yours?
Are you building and edifying?
Or spreading rumors and lying?

5.
In order to dream, you have to sleep
In order to jump, you have to leap
You have to take the proper steps
To walk in your destined success.

6.
God's behind the Potter's wheel
Allow Him to build
Let him chip away all the flaws
Give God your all.

7.
One step closer is better than not moving at all.
You have to get up in order to fall.

8.
Where are we going today?
Are we one step closer to our goals?
Does our lifestyle win over souls?
Do we practice what we preach?
Abide by what we teach?

9.
Live your life as though you are already where you want to be.
God has already fully equipped thee...

10.
Abracadabra–!
Your words are like magic.
What are you speaking into existence?

11.

Know your purpose and value
Give 100% in all that you do
Follow your dreams
Chase and pursue.

12.

Don't be the one who pours salt in an open wound
The same thing that made you laugh, will make you cry real soon.

13.

If you stay in God's grace
He'll help you win the race
Your destiny will be fulfilled
If you stay in God's will.

14.

I made it this far, I'm still here.
The past is the past, my future is near
The race has had many obstacles
With God All things are possible.

15.

Woke up today
In disarray
Then I heard a little voice say
Keep Calm and Pray.

BIOGRAPHY

Born in the mean streets of Watts, California and Raised in the Suburbs of Brentwood, California, Noel Jones takes you on a Poetic Roller Coaster ride as the two worlds collide. Read as Hope, Self-love, and Inspiration can turn around any situation.

Mission Statement:
To unite the Fire and Desire that lives within all of us.
To help Empower the lost, forgotten, and broken Souls everywhere.

www.ingramcontent.com/pod-product-compliance
Lightning Source LLC
Chambersburg PA
CBHW031531040426
42445CB00009B/489